O'Keeffe-isms

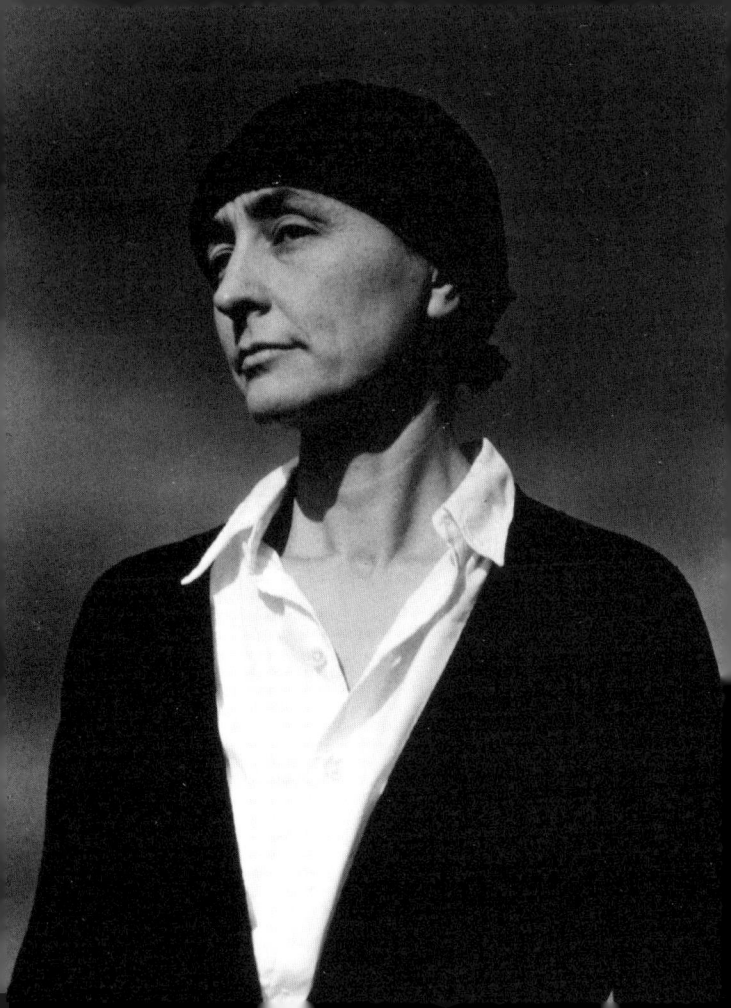

O'Keeffe-isms

Georgia O'Keeffe

Edited by Larry Warsh

PRINCETON UNIVERSITY PRESS
Princeton and Oxford

in association with
No More Rulers

Published by Princeton University Press
41 William Street, Princeton, New Jersey 08540
99 Banbury Road, Oxford OX2 6JX

press.princeton.edu
in association with
No More Rulers
nomorerulers.com
ISMs is a trademark of No More Rulers, Inc.

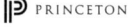 PRINCETON   NO MORE RULERS ®

GPSR Authorized Representative: Easy Access System Europe - Mustamäe
tee 50, 10621 Tallinn, Estonia, gpsr.requests@easproject.com

All Rights Reserved

ISBN 9780691284729
Library of Congress Catalog Number: 2025948262

British Library Cataloging-in-Publication Data is available
This book has been composed in Joanna MT
Printed in China

1 3 5 7 9 10 8 6 4 2

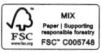

CONTENTS

INTRODUCTION

Few artists have reshaped the way we see the world around us as powerfully as Georgia O'Keeffe. From bold colors, refined forms, and a fierce sense of independence, she carved a unique place for herself in American art. Guided by a firm inner compass, she lived in a way that mirrored her art, stripped of anything not essential.

O'Keeffe declared herself an artist at an early age. Raised on a farm in rural Wisconsin, she went on to attend the School of the Art Institute of Chicago, followed by the Art Students League in New York City. She found it frustrating to copy the styles of her instructors. "If you study with anyone, you try to do what they're trying to teach you," she said.[1] "I decided that

I wasn't going to spend my life doing what had already been done."[2] Rather than joining an art movement or echoing art-world trends, she trusted her creative vision and let her own ideas shape her work. In the process, she laid a foundation for American abstract art.

O'Keeffe's creative process was rooted in and nourished by time spent in nature, specifically in the American Southwest. In her mid-twenties she took a job teaching drawing and penmanship in rural Texas. There, the rough living that would have disenchanted many others had the opposite effect—it invigorated her. She loved the open country, not as an escape from life but as a space in which to fully enter it. She loved light and its power, the shape of faraway hills, and the vast space around her. "That was my country," she said of the Texas plains. "Terrible winds and a wonderful emptiness."[3]

Soon after, O'Keeffe was introduced to the photographer and gallerist Alfred Stieglitz, a pivotal figure in her early recognition. Struck by her work, Stieglitz was responsible for many of her initial exhibitions in New York, and would later become her romantic partner. Creatively productive and personally complex, their relationship was marked by deep affection, artistic exchange, and a mutual commitment to their work. Over time, O'Keeffe stepped firmly out of Stieglitz's shadow. She valued his support but was committed to defining herself on her own terms and in her own time.

That creative exploration accelerated when O'Keeffe moved from New York to New Mexico. She returned to the city often, but rural New Mexico became her home. Her art evolved. Stones, hills, bones, and sky became the primary subjects of her work, revealing an interior landscape as expansive as the one she found in the New Mexico desert. What she painted and how she painted it came from a deeply personal place that was honest, spare, and beautiful in its refusal to explain itself.

For O'Keeffe, color was akin to music, and she composed her art accordingly. She knew what she wanted to paint before she picked up the brush. A single flower or a pelvic bone, enlarged to the point of abstraction, wasn't an object—it was a confrontation and an invitation to explore the quiet power of looking closely. "To see takes time," she said, and the desert gave her that time.[4]

Beyond her artworks, O'Keeffe left behind a trail of words—letters, interviews, artist statements, and more. Though not a professional writer, when she spoke or wrote, she did so with the same poise and precision that defined her visual work. *O'Keeffe-isms* gathers these words: her reflections on art and nature, on her life and artistic community, her process, her early feminism, and her unflinching independence. Whether you are new to Georgia O'Keeffe or have long admired her uncompromising spirit, I hope this volume brings you closer to her way of seeing: brilliant, exacting, and entirely her own.

As O'Keeffe says in these pages: "The critics can write what they please. I have already settled it for myself so flattery and criticism go down the same drain and I am quite free."[5]

LARRY WARSH
NEW YORK CITY
JULY 2025

NOTES

1 Ralph Looney, "Georgia O'Keeffe," *Atlantic*, April 1965.

2 Georgia O'Keeffe, *Georgia O'Keeffe* (New York: Viking Press, 1977).

3 Calvin Tomkins, "Georgia O'Keeffe's Vision," *New Yorker*, February 25, 1974.

4 Dorothy Seiberling, "Horizons of a Pioneer." *Life*, March 1, 1968.

5 Georgia O'Keeffe, *Georgia O'Keeffe* (New York: Viking Press, 1977).

Early Life and Artistic Awakening

My first memory is of the brightness
of light—light all around. (5)

———

I painted very little as a child, and it was
always my younger sister who was considered
the talented one. (2)

———

Learning to live is so queer. They start us out
in life with such ridiculous notions. (27)

———

My older brother was a favorite, and I can
remember comparing myself to him and
feeling I could do better. (85)

———

My mother's and my father's families had farms that adjoined and eventually my father bought mother's property. They raised all kinds of things there, even tobacco. I can still see the enormous loads of hay coming into the barns in the evening—I've never seen loads of hay like that anywhere else. (85)

———

The barn is a very healthy part of me. There should be more of it. It is something that I know … it is my childhood. (87)

———

The year I was finishing the eighth grade,
I asked our washwoman's daughter what she
was going to do when she grew up. She said
she didn't know. I said very definitively—as if
I had thought it all out and my mind was
made up—"I am going to be an artist." (5)

———

I don't really know where I got my artist
idea. The scraps of what I remember do not
explain to me where it came from. I only
know that by that time it was definitely
settled in my mind. (5)

———

I hadn't seen many pictures and I hadn't a desire to make anything like the pictures I had seen. But in one of my mother's books I had found a drawing of a girl that I thought very beautiful. The title under it was "Maid of Athens." It was a very ordinary pen-and-ink drawing about two inches high. For me, it just happened to be something special—so beautiful. … I believe that picture started something moving in me that kept on going and has had to do with the everlasting urge that makes me keep on painting. (5)

———

When people asked what kind of artist I would be, it always embarrassed me. I didn't know. Then they would ask, "Well, are you going to be an illustrator or a portrait painter or a designer, or what?" The idea of being an illustrator didn't mean much to me. I never associated my idea of being an artist with illustrations in books that we had and I didn't know what they meant by a designer. So I would say, "A portrait painter." I could grasp the idea of a portrait painter. (5)

———

I remember someone saying that if I were going to be a portrait painter I would have to paint anyone who wanted to be painted. I emphatically insisted that I only intended to paint people whom I liked or thought beautiful. (5)

———

[Commercial art was] where I learned to hurry. The idea was to do it faster or you didn't get the job. I pretty soon found out I wasn't cut out for that. It was appalling. (2)

———

Who wants to spend their life painting rabbits and copper bowls? (6)

———

The first thing I can remember drawing was a picture of a man lying on his back with his feet up in the air. ... I worked at it intensely—probably as hard as I ever worked at anything in my life. (5)

———

My mother was a great talker. She told wonderful stories. She read to us on rainy days and weekends. ... I think that reading was a good start to a lot of things. (87)

———

[My mother and I] had violent differences—we were very different kinds of people. It got so that I would not talk with her at all about many things. (15)

———

My mother and I never agreed. I got so I would just not talk about the things that I knew we would disagree about. (6)

When I was near her I tried to do what she expected—when I was alone I did as I pleased. (15)

My memories of childhood are quite pleasant, although I hated school. I left the local school when I was twelve, and was sent to a convent school in Madison. It was the one year I ever really learned anything. (87)

When I went to Chatham Episcopal Institute
in Virginia … [t]he principal was the art
teacher and the studio was my home. (5)

———

I loved the country and always on the horizon
far away was the line of the Blue Ridge
mountains—calling—as the distance has
always been calling me. (5)

———

I'd go for long walks in the woods, which
wasn't allowed. I wouldn't read my French
lesson aloud to myself three times, as we were
told to do, and in class when the teacher asked
whether I had done it I would say no—that
I didn't have the time for that. I always
had enough demerits to be expelled
if I got one more. (85)

———

I never did learn to spell. My friend
Doris Bry says now that I've ruined her
spelling because I misspell with
such confidence. (85)

————

The next year when I was at the Art
Institute of Chicago I was sent down to one
of those big galleries on the first floor to draw
casts. ... It didn't particularly interest me
but I tried to do what I thought I was
expected to do. (5)

————

Then there was a year of painting at the Art Students League in New York. ... One day someone took me into the Composition Class. ... I didn't think much of the compositions put up for criticism and I wasn't interested in what was said about them, but it started me thinking that I would try to make a painting I would really like. (5)

———

It was in the fall of 1915 that I first had the idea that what I had been taught was of little value to me except for the use of my materials as a language—charcoal, pencil, pen and ink, watercolor, pastel, and oil. (5)

———

I'd been taught to paint like other people, and I thought, what's the use? I couldn't do any better than they, or even as well. I was just adding to the brush pile. So I quit. (1)

———

I decided that I wasn't going to spend my life doing what had already been done. (5)

———

I had an important experience once. I put up everything I had done over a long period and as I looked around at my work I realized that each painting had been affected by someone else. (4)

———

I wondered why I hadn't put down things of my own from my own head. And then I realized that I hadn't done this because I'd never seen anything like the things in my own head. (4)

———

I'd always wanted to go to Texas because my mother read to us almost every night and then Sunday afternoon, and on rainy days, and I listened to all kinds of Westerns and Indian stories. (6)

———

I had a good many ideas that I'd gotten in my head when I was in the big city that I wanted to work out, and when I got out to Texas by myself I got to work on them. (6)

———

It had always seemed to me that the West must be wonderful—there was no place I knew of that I would rather go—so when I had a chance to teach there—off I went to Texas— not knowing much about teaching. (5)

———

I got so interested in teaching I wondered why I should be paid for it. (85)

———

What I enjoyed was teaching people who
had no interest in becoming artists. (85)

———

I liked to convey to [my students] the idea
that art is important in everyday life. I wanted
them to learn the principle: that when you
buy a pair of shoes or place a window in
the front of a house or address a letter or
comb your hair, consider it carefully,
so that it looks well. (90)

———

The Texas country that I know is the plains
country. It was land like the ocean all the
way around. Hardly anybody liked it,
but I loved it. (6)

———

I liked everything about Texas. I didn't even mind the dust, although sometimes when I came back from a walk I'd be the color of the road. Oh, the sun was hot and the wind was hard and you got cold in the winter—I was just crazy about all of it. (85)

———

That was my country. Terrible winds and a wonderful emptiness. (85)

———

Nature and the Desert

My world is beautiful and impossible. (55)

———

It is absurd the way I love this country. (29)

———

When I stand alone with the earth and sky a
feeling of something in me going off in every
direction into the unknown of infinity means
more to me than any thing any organized
religion gives me. (62)

———

I even get a kind of ecstasy from the vast
space—feeling like death—that is close kin to
what the male can give me—Still I have always
enjoyed it most alone—No one ever seems
equal to the country as I feel it. (68)

———

The rain makes everything such a
beautiful color. (3)

———

I lived at Lake George [New York] in the
summer for ten years. It was very pretty
but it wasn't made for me. (6)

———

Everything is so soft [in the Lake George
area]—I do not work—When the sun shines
I want to be out in it and when it is grey
I think it too dark to work. (45)

———

Here at Lake George, everything is very green.
Nothing but green. I look around and
wonder what one might paint. (6)

———

The lake is like metal—it's steaming too. (34)

———

When I got to New Mexico … [as] soon
as I saw it, that was my country. I had never
seen anything like it before but it fitted
to me exactly. (6)

———

There was nothing but sky and flat prairie
land—land that seems more like the ocean
than anything else I know. (29)

———

It was the shapes of the hills there that fasci-
nated me. The reddish sand hills with the dark
mesas behind them. It seemed as though no
matter how far you walked you could never
get into those dark hills. (85)

———

All the earth colors of the painter's palette
are out there in the many miles of bad lands.
The light Naples yellow through the ochres—
orange and red and purple earth—even
the soft earth greens. (3)

———

Stones, bones, clouds—experience gives
me shapes—but sometimes the shapes I
paint end up having no resemblance
to the actual experience. (1)

———

It is very hard to make the earth your own. (1)

———

I have almost a mania for walking. (92)

———

Wherever I go, I have an eye out for rocks. (1)

———

I walked far up into the hills—through the
woods—one morning—it occurred to me
that the thing I enjoy of the autumn is there
no matter what is happening to me—no
matter how gloomy I may be feeling. (30)

———

I was so crazy about the country that I
thought, how can I take part of it with me to
work on? There was nothing to see in the land
in the way of a flower. There were just dry
white bones. So I picked them up. (1)

———

I have wanted to paint the desert and I haven't known how. I always think that I cannot stay with it long enough. So I brought home the bleached bones as my symbols of the desert. To me they are as beautiful as anything I know. To me they are strangely more living than the animals walking around. (3)

———

I took back a barrel of bones to New York. They were my symbols of the desert, nothing more. I haven't sense enough to think of any other symbolism. The skulls were there and I could say something with them. (1)

———

The bones seem to cut sharply to the center of something that is keenly alive on the desert even though it is vast and empty and untouchable—and knows no kindness with all its beauty. (1)

———

I knew for a long time I was going to paint those bones. I had a whole pile of them in the patio waiting to be painted, and then one day I just happened to hold one up—and there was the sky through the hole. That was enough to start me. (4)

———

I was the sort of child that ate around the
raisin on the cookie and ate around the hole
in the doughnut saving either the raisin or the
hole for the last and best. So probably—not
having changed much—when I started
painting the pelvis bones I was most interested in the holes in the bones—what I saw
through them—particularly the blue from
holding them up in the sun against the sky
as one is apt to do when one seems to have
more sky than earth in one's world. (12)

———

[The bones] were most wonderful against
the Blue—that Blue that will always be
there as it is now after all man's
destruction is finished. (12)

———

[The bones] please me, and I have enjoyed them very much in relation to the sky. (6)

A pelvis bone has always been useful to any animal that has it—quite as useful as a head I suppose. (12)

The bones do not symbolize death to me. They are shapes that I enjoy. It never occurs to me that they have anything to do with death. To me they are very lively. (6)

If I could paint the flower exactly as I see it no one would see what I see because I would paint it small like the flower is small. (3)

Nobody sees a flower—really—it is so small—
we haven't the time—and to see takes time
like to have a friend takes time. (1)

———

I'll tell you how I happened to make
blown-up flowers. In the twenties, huge buildings sometimes seemed to be going up
overnight in New York. At that time I saw a
painting by Fantin-Latour, a still life with
flowers I found very beautiful, but I realized
that were I to paint the same flowers so small,
no one would look at them because I was
unknown. So I thought I'll make them big
like the huge buildings going up. People
will be startled; they'll *have* to look
at them—and they did. (4)

———

I will make even busy New Yorkers take time
to see what I see of flowers. (3)

———

I made you take time to look at what I saw,
and when you took time to really notice my
flower you hung all your own associations
with flowers on my flower, and you write
about my flower as if I think and see what you
think and see of the flower—and I don't. (85)

———

Didn't some people find sexual symbolism in your flowers?

Well, they were talking about themselves, not
about me. The people that saw them that way,
they were talking about their own self,
not about me. (6)

———

I remember someone saying to me,
"Why do you make your flowers so large?"
and I said "But you don't ask me why
I make the river so small." (6)

———

The way you see nature depends on whatever
has influenced your way of seeing. (4)

———

A flower touches almost everyone's heart.
A red hill doesn't touch everyone's heart
as it touches mine. (1)

———

You have no associations with those hills—our
waste land—I think our most beautiful
country—You may not have seen it, so you
want me always to paint flowers. I fancy this
all hasn't much to do with painting. (3)

———

The Taos country—it is so beautiful—and so
poisonous—the only way to live in it is to
strictly mind your own business. (42)

———

I hate being under a roof—it galls me
that I haven't the courage to sleep out there
in the hills alone. (44)

———

I like to see the sky when I wake and I like
the air—and I like seeing all over my
world with the rising sun. (58)

———

The Mountain calls one and the desert—and
the sagebrush—the country seems to call one
in a way that one has to answer it. (41)

———

I wish I could send you a mariposa lily—and
the smell of the damp sage—the odd dark
and bright look that comes over my world
in the low light after a little rain. (55)

———

The sky is just dripping today and it seems
I have never seen or felt anything more
perfectly quiet. (21)

———

I think of [Abiquiú] as rather a naked place—
nothing much that you can get along without—except—maybe everyone doesn't need
such fine things to look at outdoors. (15)

————

I think I've taken a bath in every brook from
Abiquiú to Española. Irrigation ditches are
fine for bathing, too. They're just wide
enough to lie down in. (85)

————

Out here, to me, the Catholic Church is like
a veil over the country, and you come across
a cross in any unexpected place. (6)

————

I have the most beautiful adobe studio—never had such a nice place all to myself—Out the very large window to a rich green alfalfa field—then the sagebrush and beyond—a most perfect mountain—it makes me feel like flying—and I don't care what becomes of Art.

(38)

———

The ranch is really home to me. I've done much less to try to make it mine. All my association with it is a kind of freedom. (1)

———

I can think of no greater luxury than being at the ranch—even if the lights didn't work and the sink wouldn't drain. (71)

———

I got tired of canned vegetables so now I grow everything I need for the year at Abiquiú. (1)

I used to think I would be cremated but now I think I'll just be put in a box and stuck in some old arroyo out there. (1)

I have no yen to go anywhere. But I go around the world anyway to see what's there—and to see if I'm in the right place. (1)

I went clear around the world flying. We were three months and a half going around, and I went halfway around again, and I still think there isn't anything better than where I live. (6)

I was flying out from the big city. The sky
looked as if you could just go out the door of
the plane and walk right out to the horizon,
the clouds looked so solid. I couldn't wait
to get home to paint it. (6)

———

What one sees from the air is so simple
and so beautiful I cannot help feeling that
it would do something wonderful for the
human race—rid it of much smallness and
pettishness if more people flew. (54)

———

It is breathtaking as one rises up over the world one has been living in—looking out at—and looks down at it stretching away and away—The Rio Grande—the mountains— Then the pattern of rivers—ridges—washes— roads—fields—water holes—wet and dry. Then little lakes—a brown pattern. Then after a while as we go over the Amarillo country a fascinating restrained pattern of different kinds of greens and cooler browns—on the square and on the bias—with a few curved shapes and many lakes. It is very handsome way off into the level distance—fantastically handsome like marvelous rug patterns— or maybe "abstract paintings." (54)

I have picked flowers where I found them—
Have picked up sea shells and rocks and
pieces of wood where there were sea shells
and rocks and pieces of wood that I liked.
When I found the beautiful white bones on
the desert I picked them up and took them
home too. I have used these things to say
what is to me the wideness and wonder
of the world as I live in it. (12)

———

Most of the human side of it isn't worth
thinking about—and as one chooses between
the country and the human being the country
becomes much more wonderful. (42)

———

I am really most fortunate that I love the sky—and the "Faraway"—and being so rich in those things. (61)

———

I believe one can have as many rare experiences at the tail end of the earth as in civilization. (78)

———

Give my greetings to the sun and the sky—and the wind—and the dry never ending land. (46)

———

Kiss the sky for me. (35)

———

Community and the
Art World

The morning is the best time[;] there are
no people around. My pleasant disposition
likes the world with nobody in it. (1)

———

I know I am unreasonable about people
but there are so many wonderful people
whom I *can't take the time* to know. (81)

———

The feeling that a person gives me
that I cannot say in words comes in
colors and shapes. (50)

———

Names of interest are what would interest
most people I suppose—It is another sort
of human quality of human nearness
and usefulness that has made what
I call my friends. (63)

———

As for my connections with people—I feel
more or less like a reed blown about by the
winds of my habits—my affections—the
things that I am. (51)

———

In the city I don't sleep well—You don't
appreciate sleeping till you haven't slept
well for a long time. (33)

———

I'm not a city person at all, but I lived in
the city for thirty years. (6)

———

I think New York is wonderful. It's like
a dream. It always makes European cities
look like villages. (6)

———

When I was first in [New York City], there
were sheep in [Central] Park. (79)

———

As I sit out here in my dry lonely country I
feel even less need for all those things that go
with the city. And while I am in the city I am
always waiting to come back here. (56)

———

If I can't work by myself for a year with no stimulus other than what I can get from books, distant friends, and for my own fun in living, I'm not worth much. (6)

———

I don't take easily to being with people. (88)

———

[Alfred Stieglitz] had to have people around, and I find people very difficult. And when I couldn't take it, I went in my room and shut the door. (6)

———

I don't know why people disturb me so much—They make me feel like a hobbled horse. (33)

———

Stieglitz liked the idea of a group.
He wanted something to come out of
America—something really important—and
he felt that you couldn't do that alone. (85)

———

[Stieglitz] was a city man and I was a
country person. (6)

———

I'll tell you what went on in my so-called mind when I did my paintings of animal skulls. There was a lot of talk in New York then—during the late twenties and early thirties—about the Great American Painting. It was like the Great American Novel. People wanted to "do" the American scene. I had gone back and forth across the country several times by then, and some of the current ideas about the American scene struck me as pretty ridiculous. To them, the American scene was a dilapidated house with a broken-down buckboard out front and a horse that looked like a skeleton. I knew America was very rich, very lush. ... For goodness' sake, I thought, the people who talk about the American scene don't know anything about it. So, in a way, that cow's skull was my joke on the American scene, and it gave me pleasure to make it in red, white, and blue. (85)

The blue and red of the bone series, it is a kind of thing that I do that makes me feel I am going off into space—in a way that I like—and that frightens me a little because it is so unlike what anyone else is doing. (57)

————

I think that what I have done is something rather unique in my time and that I am one of the few who gives our country a voice of its own—I claim no credit—it is only that I have seen with my own eye. (56)

————

Somehow, what I painted happened to fit into the emotional life of my time. (85)

————

How do you like being one of the roots of abstract American art?

Well, I must be one of the old roots. (6)

———

For me, [Stieglitz] was much more wonderful in his work than as a human being. I believe it was the work that kept me with him—though I loved him as a human being. I could see his strengths and weaknesses. I put up with what seemed to me a good deal of contradictory nonsense because of what seemed clear and bright and wonderful. (9)

———

There were always men around Stieglitz.
He had to have an audience. ... They all
thought he was wonderful for a while, then
after a while they got mad at him like
children do, you know, get mad at
their father and leave. (6)

———

Stieglitz used words in a unique, almost
violent way, which nobody has ever been able
to reproduce. It was appalling to me the way
he could tear somebody to pieces—and
that person would accept it because it
was Stieglitz talking. (85)

———

His mind was quicker than mine, of course,
but when I really knew I was right I could
often wear him down. I seldom argued with
him, though. He was the sort of person who
could be destroyed completely if you
disagreed with him. (85)

―――

For someone who moved in the world
as widely as he did, Stieglitz was something
of a child. You had to humor him a
good deal. (85)

―――

Stieglitz was a very contradictory person.
For example, he would start out in the
morning saying one thing, and by noon he
would be saying the exact opposite, and
then in the evening he would have
changed his mind again. (85)

———

The relationship that Stieglitz and I had
was really very good, because it was built
on something more than just emotional needs.
Each of us was really interested in what the
other was doing. (85)

———

I was interested in what he did, and he was interested in what I did. Very interested. So much that his favorite word was no ... to anyone who wanted anything. (6)

———

Of course, you do your best to destroy each other without knowing it—some people do it knowingly and some do it unknowingly. But if you have a real basis, as we did, you can get along pretty well despite the differences. (85)

———

I think what he did in photography was one of the great documents of the period. (85)

———

[Stieglitz] photographed my hands, he photographed me till I was crazy. (6)

———

The truth is I've been very lucky. Stieglitz was the most interesting center of energy in the art world just when I was trying to find my way. To have him get interested in me was a very good thing. (85)

———

At the time Stieglitz exhibited my drawings, no one else in New York showed that kind of thing. Many people objected to me in the beginning because I didn't fit into tradition. In those days you had to be a follower. (2)

———

I've taken a harder look at the art world than usual and it is really a strange world of people struggling after all sorts of things that have little to do with what one imagines might be called art—or anything kin to it. (72)

———

People buy pictures more through their ears than their eyes—one must be written and talked about or the people who buy through their ears think your work is not good. ... [S]o one must be written about and talked about whether one likes it or not—it always seems they say such stupid things. (69)

———

I would rather be one of the producers than one of the consumers in the human line. I would rather make the cake than eat it. (74)

———

I always have a curious sort of feeling about some of my things—I hate to show them—I am perfectly inconsistent about it—I am afraid people won't understand and—and I hope they won't—and am afraid they will. (76)

———

I can imagine myself being a much better painter and nobody paying any attention to me at all, but it happens that the things that I have done have been in touch with my time so that people have liked it. But I could have been much better and nobody noticed. (6)

———

I am often amazed at the spoken and written word telling me what I have painted. (5)

———

I don't know what Art is but I know some things it isn't when I see them. (80)

———

I don't even care much about the approbation of the Art world—its politics stink—I don't see that it matters too much. (59)

———

Prices really have no meaning—except that someone is controlling something and that they have something to control. (56)

———

My exhibition goes up today or tomorrow—It is too beautiful—I hope the next one will not be beautiful. I would like the next one to be so magnificently vulgar that all the people who have liked what I have been doing would stop speaking to me—My feeling today is that if I could do that I would be a great success to myself. (37)

A painter is one thing, and a person, in a way, is another thing. (6)

My favorite is Chinese painting. I'd still say it's the best that's been done. (85)

What happens is that you pick up ideas
here and there. If you mention any particular
source, it gives that too much emphasis. (85)

———

We probably all derive from something—with
some it is more obvious than with others—so
much so that we cannot escape a language of
line that has been growing in meaning since
the beginning of lines. (82)

———

I have been very fortunate. Much more
fortunate than most people. (6)

———

At the same time that you've said that you've been very lucky, you've also said that your life is like walking on a knife's edge.

On this knife I might fall off on either side, but I'd walk it again. So what if you do fall off. I'd rather be doing something I really wanted to do. (6)

———

Vision and Artistic Process

I have the kind of mind that transfers
experience into shapes and colors. (2)

———

Filling a space in a beautiful way.
That is what art means to me. (90)

———

There are paintings of so many things
that may be unpaintable. (50)

———

Sometimes I know where an image comes
from, sometimes not. (85)

———

From experiences of one kind or another
shapes and colors come to me very clearly—
Sometimes I start in very realistic fashion and
as I go on from one painting after another of
the same thing it becomes simplified till it can
be nothing but abstract—but for me it is my
reason for painting it I suppose. (64)

———

There are a few shapes that I have repeated
a number of times during my life and I
haven't known I was repeating them
until after I had done it. (6)

———

[My drawings] were only mine alone till
the first person saw them. (28)

———

My work—drawing—is just trying to say
something—maybe it makes me want more to
say things than most people. (94)

———

I make little drawings that have no meaning
for anyone but me. They usually get lost when
I don't need them anymore. If you saw them,
you'd wonder what those few little marks
meant, but they do mean something to me. I
don't think it matters what something comes
from; it's what you do with it that counts.
That's when it becomes yours. (4)

———

Color is one of the great things in the world that makes life worth living to me and as I have come to think of painting it is my effort to create an equivalent with paint color for the world—life as I see it. (31)

———

I see my little world—as something that I am in—something that I play in—it is inevitable to me—But I never get over being surprised that it means anything to anyone else. (30)

———

I can never show what I am working on without being stopped—Whether it is liked or disliked I am affected in the same way—sort of paralyzed. (32)

———

I see no reason why abstract and realistic art can't live side by side. The principles are the same. (2)

———

Nothing is less real than realism. Details are confusing. It is only by selection, by elimination, by emphasis, that we get at the real meaning of things. (67)

———

If you stop to think of the form—as form you are lost—The artist's form must be inevitable—You mustn't even think you won't succeed. (32)

———

Whether you succeed or not is irrelevant—
There is no such thing—Making your unknown known is the important thing. (32)

———

Painting isn't just putting the paint on. (79)

———

Making the unknown—known—in terms of
one's medium is all absorbing. (32)

———

The subject matter of a painting should never
obscure its form and color, which are its real
thematic contents. ... So I have no difficulty in
contending that my paintings of a flower may
be just as much a product of this age as a
cartoon about the freedom of women—or
the working class—or anything else. (84)

———

I'm always swinging from one thing to the other. I have always been very free in my approach. (2)

———

Often, a picture just gets into my head without my having the least idea how it got there. But I'm much more down-to-earth than people give me credit for. At times, I'm ridiculously realistic. (85)

———

The large White Flower with the golden heart is something I have to say about White—quite different from what White has been meaning to me. Whether the flower or the color is the focus I do not know. I do know that the flower is painted large to convey to you my experience of the flower—and what is my experience of the flower if it is not color. (43)

You paint from your subject, not what you see, so you can't be bothered with changes in light. (4)

I had to create an equivalent for what I felt about what I was looking at—not copy it. (5)

I rarely paint anything I don't know very well. (4)

I'm one of the few artists, maybe the only one today, who is willing to talk about my work as pretty. I don't mind it being pretty. I think it's a shame to discard this word; maybe if we work on it hard enough we can make it fashionable again. (4)

I never was that interested in doing people. It was very easy with drawings for me to get a likeness, but that wasn't any particular fun to me. (6)

I've had to pose for too many people myself. It's a hard business and I haven't what it takes to ask someone else to do this for me. (4)

―――――

I rarely start anything that isn't pretty clear to me before I start. I know what I'm going to do before I begin, and if there's nothing in my head, I do nothing. Work brings work for me. (4)

―――――

It is very hard work to turn out anything that looks like a good painting. I seem to be busy all day from six o'clock on and I don't get much done. (3)

―――――

What Is Art? I'm beginning to think that
maybe I'm exceedingly vulgar—and the funny
thing about it is—I don't understand—I get
the shapes in my head—can never make them
exactly like I want to—but there is a fascina-
tion about trying—And then too—there is
the delicious probability that I don't know
anything about what Art is—So it's fun
to make the stuff. (65)

―――――

I always feel that sometimes I may fall off
the edge—It is something I like so much to
do that I don't care if I do fall off the edge—
No sense in it but it is my way. (57)

―――――

I can see shapes. It's as if my mind
creates shapes that I don't know about.
I get this shape in my head, and sometimes
I know what it comes from and
sometimes I don't. (6)

For most people a show is a joy; for me
it's a bore, a headache, and it's the kind of
work an artist shouldn't be doing. (4)

I mentally destroy the pictures I look at.
I'm very critical. I don't seem to have the
kind of pleasure I know a lot of other
people have in pictures. (85)

A painting is like a person. You either
like it or you don't. (91)

I am not saying that it takes time to understand a painting because at present I am
inclined to think that rather unimportant—
maybe impossible—as it seems quite
impossible for two people to really
understand one another. (48)

What can you do if people who own
your pictures are willing to lend them to any
exhibition? I was in a surrealist show when I'd
never heard of surrealism. I'm not a joiner and
I'm not a precisionist or anything else. (4)

Did you ever have something to say, and feel as if the whole side of the wall wouldn't be big enough to say it on? (22)

———

I like an empty wall because I can imagine what I like on it. (81)

———

I like to have things as sparse as possible. If you have an empty wall, you can think on it better. I like a space to think in—if you can call what I do thinking. (85)

———

My brain feels like an old scrapbag—all sorts of pieces of all sorts of things. (24)

———

Making order in the debris of so many
years takes a long time—I destroy everything
of my own that I can—as I go—intending
to leave as small a chore as possible
when I take off. (86)

———

My house in Abiquiú is pretty empty; only
what I need is in it. I like walls empty. (4)

———

Possessions are such a headache. I've often
thought how wonderful it would be to simply
stand out in space and have nothing! (2)

———

The idea of death makes "things" seem so unimportant—one has the use of them for such a short period of time. (73)

———

Other people always put the names on my pictures—quite funny names I think. I don't think it's necessary. (2)

———

The meaning of a word—to me—is not as exact as the meaning of a color. Colors and shapes make a more definite statement than words. (5)

———

Words and I—are not good friends at all
except with some people. (18)

———

The painter using the word often seems
to me like a child trying to walk. (19)

———

I do not care for poetry. It is almost a
complete blind spot for me. (7)

———

I think I'd rather let the painting work for
itself than help it with the word. (19)

———

If there is any personal quality in [my paintings], then that will be signature enough. (2)

———

What is Art—anyway? When I think of how hopelessly unable I am to answer that question I cannot help feeling like a farce. (21)

———

I wonder if I am a raving lunatic for trying to make these things—You know— I don't care if I am—but I do wonder sometimes. (22)

———

The uncertain feeling that some of my ideas may be near insanity—adds to the fun of it. (25)

———

When one begins to wander around in one's own thoughts and half-thoughts what one sees is often surprising. (11)

———

I feel that insanity might be a luxury. (75)

———

I rather think time and painting haven't much in common and will have to get along without one another. (48)

———

[Painting is] like a thread that runs through
all the reasons for all the other things
that make one's life. (85)

———

Artists and religionists are never far apart[;]
they go to the sources of revelation for what
they choose to experience and what they
report is the degree of their experiences. (14)

———

Intellect wishes to arrange—intuition
wishes to accept. (14)

———

My painting is what I have to give back to the
world for what the world gives to me. (66)

———

Why bring into the world less than the
most beautiful thing you can. (47)

———

"Go home and work." That's all I can
tell anyone. (85)

Womanhood
and Independence

I was made to work hard. (23)

———

You decide on the kind of person you want
to be, and then you get at it. It's like a habit
of neatness. (2)

———

I grew up pretty much as everybody else grows up and one day found myself saying to myself—I can't live where I want to—I can't go where I want to—I can't do what I want to—I can't even say what I want to—School and things that painters have taught me even keep me from painting as I want to. I decided I was a very stupid fool not to at least paint as I wanted to and say what I wanted to when I painted as that seemed to be the only thing I could do that didn't concern anybody but myself—that was nobody's business but my own. (10)

———

I have always been willing to bet on myself you know—and been willing to stand on what I am and can do even when the world isn't much with me. (59)

My feeling about life is a curious kind of triumphant feeling about—seeing it black—knowing it is so and walking into it fearlessly.

(42)

If you knew how very much afraid I am to say and do things sometimes—you would think my nerve in doing them almost inexcusable—It is one of the strongest symptoms of insanity I have—but life wouldn't be worth living to me without it. (95)

The surface doings of the days are only important in so far as they do something for an undercurrent that seems to be running very strong in me—As I can't tell where it is going—all I can say is that I am enjoying the way. (39)

———

I never cared anything at all what other people thought. I always knew I could earn a living doing something else besides painting, so I wasn't worried. (85)

———

I do not like the idea of happiness—it is too momentary—I would say that I was always busy and interested in something— interest has more meaning to me than the idea of happiness. (15)

———

I like to be interested. And I paint what
interests me. If I could be ten people, I'd keep
them all running all day. I like to do things.
I like to go places. Yes, I live here in a
rather isolated fashion, but now
and then I take a trip. (2)

———

There are so many things to do and see!
I think if I have a next life I would like to
sing in it. I love music. (2)

———

Singing has always seemed to me the
most perfect means of expression. Since
I cannot sing, I paint. (13)

———

I like [music] better than anything in the world—Color gives me the same thrill once in a long long time—I can almost remember and count the times. (21)

———

I have a single-track mind. I work on an idea for a long time. It's like getting acquainted with a person, and I don't get acquainted easily. (4)

———

No matter what failure or success we may have—we will not know—But we can keep our own integrity—according to our own sense of balance with the world. (32)

———

What others have called form has nothing to do with our form—I want to create my own. (32)

———

I don't start until I'm almost entirely clear. It's a waste of time and paint. (6)

———

I feel that my world is a rock—When a very prominent catholic priest—he was head of the chemistry [department] at Fordham—tried to convert me to the catholic church—I was amazed that he could only make the catholic church seem like a mound of jelly compared to my rock. (59)

———

I think one of my best times was when nobody was interested in me. That may have come from my not being the favorite child in the family, and not minding that I wasn't—it left me very free. (85)

———

I thought someone could tell me how to paint a landscape, but I never found that person. … [T]hey could tell you how they painted their landscape but they couldn't tell me to paint mine. (6)

———

It seems to me very important to the idea of true democracy—to my country—and to the world eventually—that all men and women stand equal under the sky. (17)

———

I have always resented being told that there are
things I cannot do because I am a woman. (16)

———

At first the men didn't want me around. They
couldn't take a woman artist seriously. (1)

———

Men in that day didn't want women painting.
The painters and the art patrons figured it
was strictly a man's world. (2)

———

The men decided they didn't want me
to paint New York. They wouldn't let me.
They told me to "leave New York to
the men." I was furious! (2)

———

I just feel I'm bound to seem all wrong most of the time, so there's nothing to do but walk ahead and make the best of it. (89)

———

The men were all talking about the Great American Novel, the Great American Play, oh it was the Great American everything. And I thought they didn't know anything about America—a lot of them have never been across the Hudson. (6)

———

The men didn't like my color. My color was hopeless. My color was too bright. ... I thought what most of them used was pretty dirty. (6)

———

I got along with [the other artists in Stieglitz's circle] very well, because I did all the hard work for them. I hung up their shows, and carried their pictures around, and put them in storage, and got them out. I was quite a useful citizen. (6)

———

I was never called Miss before. In Stieglitz's days, I was always just called by my last name. Stieglitz called me Georgia, but the others just called me O'Keeffe. But I was never called Miss O'Keeffe. (79)

———

I feel like a little plant that [Stieglitz] has
watered and weeded and dug around—and he
seems to have been able to grow himself—
without anyone watering or weeding or
digging around him. (36)

———

My center does not come from my mind—it
feels in me like a plot of warm moist well
tilled earth with the sun shining hot on it—
nothing with a spark of possibility of growth
seems seeded in it at the moment—It seems I
would rather feel it starkly empty than let
anything be planted that cannot be tended to
the fullest possibility of growth. (49)

———

It was nice of Stieglitz to let you go to New Mexico every summer.

Well, listen, he didn't let me go. I just went. (6)

I've taken hold of anything that came along that I wanted. (6)

A woman who has lived many things and who sees lines and colors as an expression of living—might say something that a man can't. (35)

I feel there is something unexplored about woman that only a woman can explore. (35)

The [painting] seems to express in a way what I want it to but—it also seems rather effeminate—it is essentially a woman's feeling—satisfies me in a way—I don't know whether the fault is with the execution or with what I tried to say. ... There are things we want to say—but saying them is pretty nervy. (23)

———

I wonder if man has ever been written down the way he has written woman down—I rather feel that he hasn't been. (32)

———

I am so sure that Work is the thing in life—and we mustn't let the human problems kill us. (41)

———

[Painting] seemed to be the only thing
that I could do that did not concern
anyone but myself. (13)

———

I get out my work and have a show for myself
before I have it publicly. I make up my own
mind about it—how good or bad or indiffer-
ent it is. After that the critics can write what
they please. I have already settled it for myself
so flattery and criticism go down the same
drain and I am quite free. (5)

———

It is as if I have a strange oily skin of some sort
that words don't get through at the time they
might disturb me—they don't seem to get
through till I think them funny. (53)

———

If I stop to think of what others—authorities or the public—or anyone—would say of my form I'd not be able to do anything. (32)

———

The things [the critics] write sound so strange and far removed from what I feel of myself. They make me seem like some strange unearthly sort of a creature floating in the air—breathing in clouds for nourishment—when the truth is that I like beef steak—and like it rare at that. (8)

———

I believe in women making their own living. It will be nice when women have equal opportunities and status with men so that it is taken as a matter of course. I think there are some men who would like to cook and keep house. Why shouldn't they? (60)

———

Equal Rights and Responsibilities is a basic idea that would have very important psychological effects on women and men from the time they are born. It could very much change the girl child's idea of her place in the world. (17)

———

I would like each child to feel responsible
for the country and that no door for any
activity they may choose is closed on
the account of sex. (17)

———

Often I've had the feeling that I could have
been a much better painter and had far less
recognition. It's just that what I do seems to
move people today, in a way that I don't
understand at all. (85)

———

Now and then when I get an idea for a
picture, I think, How ordinary. Why paint that
old rock? Why not go for a walk instead?
But then I realize that to someone else
it may not seem ordinary. (85)

———

One's truth must always necessarily have
a certain amount of fantasy in it—I think the
human being functions that way—but the
fantasy must be one's truth to keep one's
whole consistent—It must be your
real experience. (47)

———

The world just seems to be on wheels—going
so fast I can't see the spokes—and I like it. (26)

———

I want to hurry up and live fast—because
I want to know—and the only way I can
find out is by living. (93)

———

Living is so difficult. (33)

———

I want to love as hard as I can. (24)

———

The summer had brought me to a state of
mind where I felt as grateful for my largest
hurts as I did for my largest happiness. (40)

———

Each day is perfect in its way. (39)

———

If you work hard enough, you can get
almost anything. ... I got [the Abiquiú House]
away from the Catholic Church and
that's an achievement. (6)

———

I got around. I didn't miss much of anything.
(6)

———

What is the difference whether I win or
lose—I am a very small moment in time. (59)

———

I'm disgusted with dreams now—I want real
things—live people to take hold of—to see—
and to talk to—Music that makes
holes in the sky. (24)

———

I'm glad I want everything in the world—
good and bad—bitter and sweet—I want
it all and a lot of it too. (20)

———

Try to keep what is beautiful to you and
what you can use for today and now—You
must not let the things you cannot
help destroy you. (41)

———

Do save your strength and energy for
creating—don't spend it on problems and
situations you can't help. (41)

———

I like the artist standing up for himself—
believing in his own word no matter what
anyone may say about it. Believing in what
one does oneself is really more important than
having other people pat you on the back. (52)

———

It always seems to me that so few people live—
they just seem to exist and I don't see any
reason why we shouldn't *live always*—till
we die physically. (77)

———

I think more about tomorrow than today
or yesterday. I'm not a regretter. (1)

———

*Where do you suppose you got the idea of being
an artist?*

I haven't the faintest idea. I often think
about it and wonder. (6)

———

If you can believe in what you are and
keep to your line—that is the most one
can do with life. (70)

———

Where I was born and where and how
I have lived is unimportant. It is what I have
done with where I have been that
should be of interest. (5)

———

My life is good—and I like it. The dog and
I have a walk almost every early morning and
again at sunset—He just now banged on the
door to tell me he was ready to come
in and go to bed. (83)

———

I'm frightened all the time. Scared to death.
But I've never let it stop me. Never! (91)

———

SOURCES

1. Seiberling, Dorothy. "Horizons of a Pioneer." Life, March 1, 1968.
2. Looney, Ralph. "Georgia O'Keeffe." *Atlantic*, April 1965.
3. O'Keeffe, Georgia. "About Myself." Announcement for *Exhibition of Oils and Pastels* at An American Place held January 22–March 17, 1939. Accessed via *The Met: Watson Library Digital Collections*, b18338276.
4. Kuh, Katharine. *The Artist's Voice: Talks with Seventeen Artists.* New York: Harper and Row, 1962.
5. O'Keeffe, Georgia. *Georgia O'Keeffe.* New York: Viking Press, 1977.
6. Adato, Perry Miller, dir. *Georgia O'Keeffe.* 1977.
7. Dijkstra, Bram. "America and Georgia O'Keeffe." In *Georgia O'Keeffe: The New York Years*, edited by Doris Bry and Nicholas Callaway, 105–29. New York: Alfred A. Knopf, 1991.
8. O'Keeffe, Georgia. "Letter to Mitchell Kennerley, NY" (Fall 1922). In *Arts and Letters*, edited by Jack Cowart and Juan Hamilton, with letters selected and annotated by Sarah Greenough, 170–71. Washington, DC: National Gallery of Art, 1988. Further references to this source are given as *AL*, followed by the page number(s).
9. O'Keeffe, Georgia. Introduction to *Georgia O'Keeffe: A Portrait*

by *Alfred Stieglitz*, unpaginated. New York: Metropolitan Museum of Art, 1978.

10. O'Keeffe, Georgia. Catalog statement for *Alfred Stieglitz Presents One Hundred Pictures: Oils, Water-Colors, Pastels, Drawings by Georgia O'Keeffe, American*. New York: Anderson Galleries, 1923. Reprinted in *Georgia O'Keeffe: An Exhibition of the Work of the Artist from 1915 to 1966*, edited by Mitchell A. Wilder. Fort Worth: Amon Carter Museum, 1966.

11. O'Keeffe, Georgia. *Some Memories of Drawings*. Edited by Doris Bry. Albuquerque: University of New Mexico Press, 1974.

12. O'Keeffe, Georgia. "About Painting Desert Bones." Announcement for *Georgia O'Keeffe: Paintings—1943 at An American Place*, January 11–March 11, 1944.

13. "Austere Stripper." *Time*, May 27, 1946.

14. Scott, Gail R. *Marsden Hartley*. New York: Cross River Press, 1988, 167.

15. Giboire, Clive, ed. Afterword to *Lovingly, Georgia: The Complete Correspondence of Georgia O'Keeffe & Anita Pollitzer*, edited by Clive Giboire, 323–25. New York: Simon and Schuster, 1990. Further references to this source are given as *LG*, followed by the page number(s).

16. O'Keeffe, Georgia. Address to National Woman's Party, 1926.

17. O'Keeffe, Georgia. "Letter from Georgia O'Keeffe to Eleanor Roosevelt." In *AL* (2/10/1944).

18. O'Keeffe, Georgia. "Letter to Alfred Stieglitz, Columbia, SC" (2/1/1916). In *My Faraway One: Selected Letters of Georgia O'Keeffe and Alfred Stieglitz*, edited by Sarah Greenough, 4–5. New Haven: Yale University Press, 2011. Further references to this source are given as MFO, followed by the page number(s).

19. Greenough, Sarah. "From the Faraway." In *AL*, 135–39.

20. O'Keeffe. "Letter to Anita Pollitzer, Charlottesville, VA" (8/25/1915). In *LG*, 14–17.

21. O'Keeffe. "Letter to Anita Pollitzer, Columbia, SC" (10/1915). In *LG*, 59–61.

22. O'Keeffe. "Letter to Anita Pollitzer, Columbia, SC" (12/1915). In *LG*, 103.

23. O'Keeffe. "Letter to Anita Pollitzer, Columbia, SC" (1/4/1916). In *AL*, 147–48.

24. O'Keeffe. "Letter to Anita Pollitzer, Columbia, SC" (1/14/1916). In *AL*, 149.

25. O'Keeffe. "Letter to Alfred Stieglitz, Columbia, SC" (2/1/1916). In *AL*, 150.

26. O'Keeffe. "Letter to Anita Pollitzer, Columbia, SC" (2/9/1916). In *AL*, 151.

27. O'Keeffe. "Letter to Anita Pollitzer, Columbia, SC" (2/21/1916). In *AL*, 152.

28. O'Keeffe. "Letter to Alfred Stieglitz, Charlottesville, VA" (7/27/1916). In *AL*, 153–54.

29. O'Keeffe. "Letter to Anita Pollitzer, Canyon, TX" (9/11/1916). In *AL*, 156–57.

30. O'Keeffe. "Letter to Mitchell Kennerley, NY" (1/20/1929). In *AL*, 187.

31. Milliken, William M. "White Flower by Georgia O'Keeffe." *Bulletin of the Cleveland Museum of Art*, April 1937.

32. O'Keeffe. "Letter to Sherwood Anderson, Lake George, NY" (9/1923). In *AL*, 173–75.

33. O'Keeffe. "Letter to Sherwood Anderson, Lake George, NY" (6/11/1924). In *AL*, 177–78.

34. O'Keeffe. "Letter to Sherwood Anderson, Lake George, NY" (11/1924). In *AL*, 178–79.

35. O'Keeffe. "Letter to Mabel Dodge Luhan, NY" (1925). In *AL*, 180.

36. O'Keeffe. "Letter to Blanche Matthias, NY" (1926). In *AL*, 183.

37. O'Keeffe. "Letter to Waldo Frank, NY" (1/10/1927). In *AL*, 184–85.

38. O'Keeffe. "Letter to Henry McBride, Taos, NM" (Summer 1929). In *AL*, 189–90.

39. O'Keeffe. "Letter to Mabel Dodge Luhan, Taos, NM" (6/1929). In *AL*, 191.

40. O'Keeffe. "Letter to Mabel Dodge Luhan, Lake George, NY" (9/1929). In *AL*, 196.

41. O'Keeffe. "Letter to Dorothy Brett, NY" (4/1930). In *AL*, 200.

42. O'Keeffe. "Letter to Dorothy Brett, NY" (10/1930). In *AL*, 201.

43. O'Keeffe. "Letter to William Milliken, NY" (11/1/1930). In *AL*, 202.

44. O'Keeffe. "Letter to Henry McBride, Alcalde, NM" (7/1931). In *AL*, 202–3.

45. O'Keeffe. "Letter to Henry McBride, Lake George, NY" (late 8/1931). In *AL*, 204.

46. O'Keeffe. "Letter to Russell Vernon Hunter, NY" (Spring 1932). In *AL*, 207.

47. O'Keeffe. "Letter to Dorothy Brett" (1932). In *AL*, 207–10.

48. O'Keeffe. "Letter to Russell Vernon Hunter, NY" (early 2/1933). In *AL*, 211–12.

49. O'Keeffe. "Letter to Jean Toomer, Lake George, NY" (1/10/1934). In *AL*, 217–18.

50. O'Keeffe. "Letter to Jean Toomer, Lake George, NY" (2/8/1934). In *AL*, 218–19.

51. O'Keeffe. "Letter to Jean Toomer" (3/1934). In *AL*, 219–20.

52. O'Keeffe. "Letter to Cady Wells, NY" (late 2/1938). In *AL*, 224.

53. O'Keeffe. "Letter to Henry McBride, NY" (7/22/1939). In *AL*, 228–29.

54. O'Keeffe. "Letter to Maria Chabot, NY" (11/17/1941). In *Maria Chabot—Georgia O'Keeffe: Correspondence, 1941–1949*,

edited by Barbara Buhler Lynes and Ann Paden, 12–13. Albuquerque: University of New Mexico Press, 2003. Further references to this source are given as MC, followed by the page number(s).

55. O'Keeffe. "Letter to Maude and Frederick Mortimer Clapp, Abiquiú, NM" (6/9/1945). In *AL*, 239–40.

56. O'Keeffe. "Letter to James Johnson Sweeney, Abiquiú, NM" (6/11/1945). In *AL*, 240–42.

57. O'Keeffe. "Letter to Caroline Fesler, NY" (12/24/1945). In *AL*, 242–43.

58. O'Keeffe. "Letter to Henry McBride, Abiquiú, NM" (7/19/1948). In *AL*, 247–48.

59. O'Keeffe. "Letter to William Howard Schubart, Abiquiú, NM" (7/28/1950). In *AL*, 253–54.

60. Taylor, Carol. "Lady Dynamo: Miss O'Keeffe, Noted Artist, Is a Feminist." *New York World-Telegram*, March 31, 1945.

61. O'Keeffe. "Letter to William Howard Schubart, Abiquiú, NM" (1/19/1951). In *AL*, 258–60.

62. O'Keeffe. "Letter to William Howard Schubart, Abiquiú, NM" (7/25/1952). In *AL*, 262–63.

63. O'Keeffe. "Letter to Anita Pollitzer, Abiquiú, NM" (10/24/1955). In *AL*, 264–65.

64. O'Keeffe. "Letter to John I. H. Baur, Abiquiú, NM" (4/22/1957). In *AL*, 266–67.

65. O'Keeffe. "Letter to Alfred Stieglitz, Canyon, TX" (11/12/1916). In *MFO*, 66–73.

66. "Pineapple for Papaya." *Time*, February 12, 1940.

67. "I Can't Sing, So I Paint! Says Ultra Realistic Artist; Art Is Not Photography—It Is Expression of Inner Life! Miss Georgia O'Keeffe Explains Subjective Aspect of Her Work." *Sun*, December 5, 1922.

68. O'Keeffe. "Letter to Alfred Stieglitz, Lake George, NY" (11/20/1932). In MFO, 663.

69. O'Keeffe. "Letter to Doris McMurdo, Lake George, NY" (7/1/1922). In *AL*, 169–70.

70. O'Keeffe. "Letter to Maria Chabot, NY" (1/10/1944). In MC, 160–61.

71. O'Keeffe. "Letter to Maria Chabot, NY" (12/9/1944). In MC, 221–22.

72. O'Keeffe. "Letter to Maria Chabot, NY" (1/9/1945). In MC, 234–35.

73. O'Keeffe. "Letter to Maria Chabot, NY" (2/15/1945). In MC, 246–47.

74. O'Keeffe. "Letter to Maria Chabot, NY" (2/21/1945). In MC, 250–51.

75. O'Keeffe. "Letter to Anita Pollitzer, Columbia, SC" (9/1915). In *LG*, 32–33.

76. O'Keeffe. "Letter to Anita Pollitzer, Columbia, SC" (10/1915). In *LG*, 46–49.

77. O'Keeffe. "Letter to Anita Pollitzer, Columbia, SC" (10/1915). In *LG*, 52–53.

78. O'Keeffe. "Letter to Anita Pollitzer, Columbia, SC" (10/1915). In *LG*, 58–59.

79. Warhol, Andy. "Georgia O'Keeffe & Juan Hamilton." *Interview*, September 1983.

80. O'Keeffe. "Letter to Anita Pollitzer, Canyon, TX" (10/1915). In *LG*, 248–49.

81. Pollitzer, Anita. "That's Georgia." In *LG*, 289–95.

82. O'Keeffe. "Letter to Anita Pollitzer, Abiquiú, NM" (1/17/1956). In *LG*, 305.

83. O'Keeffe. "Letter to Anita Pollitzer, Abiquiú, NM" (10/20/1958). In *LG*, 317–18.

84. Robinson, Roxana. "Chapter 22." In *Georgia O'Keeffe: A Life*. Waltham: Brandeis University Press, 1989, 346–64. Further references to this source are given as *GO*, followed by the page number(s).

85. Tomkins, Calvin. "Georgia O'Keeffe's Vision." *New Yorker*, February 25, 1974.

86. O'Keeffe. "Letter to Maria Chabot, NY" (2/7/1948). In *MC*, 441.

87. Robinson. "Chapter 2." In *GO*, 14–25.

88. Robinson. "Chapter 3." In *GO*, 26–35.

89. Robinson. "Chapter 4." In *GO*, 37–45.

90. Robinson. "Chapter 9." In *GO*, 85–94.

91. Kotz, Mary Lynn. "Georgia O'Keeffe at 90." *Artnews*, December 1977.

92. Robinson. "Chapter 11." In *GO*, 111–30.

93. Robinson. "Chapter 12." In *GO*, 131–51.

94. O'Keeffe. "Letter to Arthur McMahon" (2/8/1916). In *GO*, 655–56.

95. O'Keeffe. "Letter to Arthur McMahon" (9/4/1915). In *GO*, 641–42.

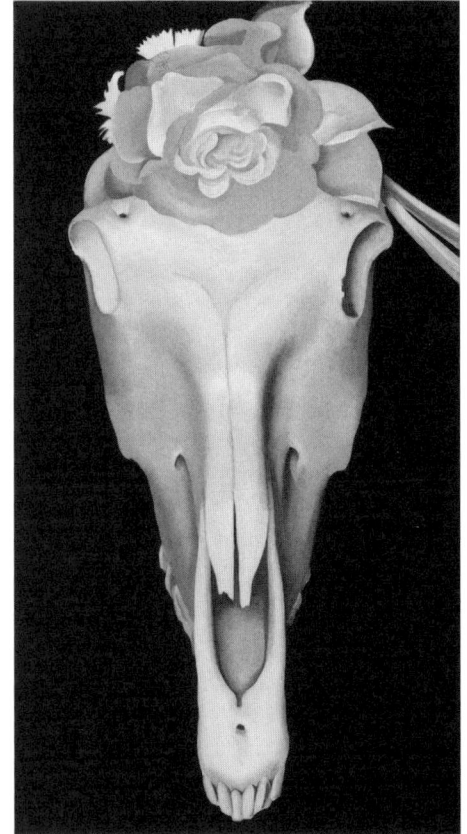

CHRONOLOGY

1887

November 15: Georgia Totto O'Keeffe is born to Francis Calyxtus O'Keeffe and Ida (Totto) O'Keeffe near Sun Prairie, Wisconsin. She is the second of seven children.

1898

O'Keeffe begins private drawing lessons with her two younger sisters under the instruction of Sarah Mann. Later that year, she begins watercolor lessons.

1901

O'Keeffe begins receiving formal art education at Sacred Heart Academy boarding school in Madison, Wisconsin, approximately twenty miles from Sun Prairie.

1902

O'Keeffe's family moves to Williamsburg, Virginia. She remains with her aunt in Madison.

1903

O'Keeffe joins her family in Williamsburg and enrolls
as a boarding student at Chatham Episcopal Institute
in Chatham, Virginia, majoring in art.

1905

O'Keeffe graduates from high school.
In the fall, O'Keeffe begins attending the School of the
Art Institute of Chicago.

1907

O'Keeffe attends the Art Students League in New York
City, studying under William Merritt Chase.

1908

O'Keeffe visits Alfred Stieglitz's gallery 291 to see
drawings of French artist Auguste Rodin.
After receiving the esteemed Chase Award, O'Keeffe
attends Amitola, the Art Students League's outdoor
school in Lake George, New York, for the summer.

O'Keeffe works as a freelance commercial artist for Little Dutch Girl Cleanser in Chicago.

1910

O'Keeffe contracts measles and moves to Charlottesville, Virginia, to join her mother and siblings.

1911

O'Keeffe takes her first teaching position at Chatham Episcopal Institute.

1912

O'Keeffe attends a summer class for art teachers at the University of Virginia taught by Alon Bement from Teachers College, Columbia University, in New York City. He introduces her to Arthur Wesley Dow's ideas of abstract and harmonious compositions.

O'Keeffe accepts a position as head of the art department in the Amarillo, Texas, public school district (1912–14).

1913

O'Keeffe begins a three-year stint working summers as the teaching assistant for Bement at the University of Virginia.

1914

O'Keeffe begins attending Dow's classes at Teachers College.

O'Keeffe teaches at Columbia College, South Carolina.

O'Keeffe joins the National Woman's Party on behalf of women's suffrage and maintains her membership for many decades.

1915

February 4: O'Keeffe opens the first public showing of her artwork. Her painting *Scarlet Sage* is included in the annual exhibition of the American Watercolor Society at the National Arts Club in New York City.

O'Keeffe reads Wassily Kandinsky's book *Concerning the Spiritual in Art*.

O'Keeffe teaches at Columbia College, South Carolina.

1916

January 1: Anita Pollitzer, a friend of the artist, shows O'Keeffe's abstract drawings to Stieglitz. He exhibits ten charcoal drawings on May 23 at 291.

May 1: Georgia O'Keeffe's mother dies of tuberculosis.

August: O'Keeffe moves to Canyon, Texas, to become head of the art department at West Texas State Normal College. She and Stieglitz begin a personal correspondence.

1917

April 3: O'Keeffe travels to New York for her first one-woman show at 291. Her first sale is *Train at Night in the Desert* from 1916 ($400). Stieglitz begins his photographic portraiture of O'Keeffe.

May 25–June 1: O'Keeffe travels to New York City and meets Paul Strand and the Stieglitz circle.

August: O'Keeffe and her sister Claudia stop in Santa Fe, New Mexico, en route to Colorado, her first trip to the area.

1918

February: O'Keeffe moves to San Antonio, Texas, to recover from a respiratory illness.

June: O'Keeffe accepts Stieglitz's invitation to paint in New York City for one year with his financial support.

August: O'Keeffe makes her first visit to Stieglitz's family home in Lake George.

November 6: O'Keeffe's father dies.

1919

At Lake George, O'Keeffe begins painting small-scale canna lilies with cropped and magnified compositions.

1920

August: O'Keeffe refurbishes a shed at Lake George to use as a studio.

1921

February: Anderson Galleries presents its first exhibition of Stieglitz's intimate photographs of O'Keeffe.

1922

October: Paul Rosenfeld publishes an article on
O'Keeffe's upcoming exhibition at Anderson
Galleries in *Vanity Fair*.

1923

January 29: Stieglitz organizes the first annual solo
exhibition of O'Keeffe's artwork, and O'Keeffe's
second solo exhibition ever, at Anderson Galleries;
this continues yearly until his death in 1946.

1924

March: O'Keeffe and Stieglitz exhibit their work
together at Anderson Galleries.

November: O'Keeffe and Stieglitz move into their first
home, Thirty-Five East Fifty-Eighth Street in New
York City.

December 11: Stieglitz and O'Keeffe are married by a
justice of the peace in Cliffside Park, New Jersey.

O'Keeffe begins to create large-scale flower paintings.

1925

March 9: Stieglitz's exhibition *Seven Americans* opens at Anderson Galleries, including works by him, Arthur Dove, Marsden Hartley, John Marin, Charles Demuth, Paul Strand, and Georgia O'Keeffe.

November: O'Keeffe and Stieglitz move into the Shelton Hotel, the first skyscraper residence in New York City. From her window, O'Keeffe begins to paint images of the cityscape.

December: Stieglitz opens the Intimate Gallery, a space dedicated to American modernism. O'Keeffe exhibits her works in annual shows and supervises all gallery installations.

1926

February: O'Keeffe addresses the National Woman's Party convention in Washington, DC.

1927

June 1–September 1: The Brooklyn Museum of Art hosts its first exhibition of O'Keeffe's art, *Paintings by Georgia O'Keeffe*.

July: O'Keeffe undergoes surgery for breast cancer.

1929

April–August: O'Keeffe travels to New Mexico with
Rebecca Salisbury Strand, spending her first summer
in Taos, New Mexico, at the home of Mabel Dodge
Luhan.

December 13: Five of O'Keeffe's paintings are included
in *Paintings by Nineteen Living Americans*, the second
exhibition ever to be held at the recently opened
Museum of Modern Art.

1930

February–March: Paintings from New Mexico are
exhibited for the first time at An American Place
gallery along with O'Keeffe's urban and floral
imagery.

June–September: O'Keeffe returns to Taos for a second
summer as Luhan's guest.

1931

April: O'Keeffe visits New Mexico for the third time and rents a cottage in Alcalde at the H&M Ranch owned by Marie Tudor Garland; she begins to paint skulls and bones as isolated objects in the tradition of still life painting.

1932

Summer: O'Keeffe stays at Lake George with Stieglitz instead of going to New Mexico.

August 1932: O'Keeffe travels in the Gaspé area of Canada (eastern Quebec) and is inspired to paint landscapes, barns, and crosses.

1933

O'Keeffe is diagnosed with psychoneurosis and spends two months at Doctors Hospital in New York. She recuperates with friends in Bermuda and spends the summer at Lake George.

1934

June: O'Keeffe returns to New Mexico for the first
time since 1931 and visits Ghost Ranch, where she
paints high desert land formations.

The Metropolitan Museum of Art purchases its first
O'Keeffe painting, *Black Hollyhock, Blue Larkspur*
(1929).

1935

The Whitney Museum of American Art opens the
exhibition *Abstract Painting in America*, including five
paintings by O'Keeffe.

O'Keeffe paints her first image combining bones,
flowers, and the landscape of Ghost Ranch.

1936

April: O'Keeffe and Stieglitz move into an apartment
at 405 East Fifty-Fourth Street in New York City.

O'Keeffe begins painting 150 miles west of Ghost Ranch
at a site she calls the "Black Place," the Bisti Badlands
in the Navajo Nation.

1937

O'Keeffe stays in an adobe house at Ghost Ranch, owned
by Arthur Pack.

1938

February: *Life* magazine publishes a four-page spread
with photographs by Ansel Adams, proclaiming
O'Keeffe the "country's most prosperous and talked-
of painters."

O'Keeffe receives an honorary Doctor of Fine Arts degree
from the College of William and Mary in Virginia, the
first of many similar awards.

O'Keeffe travels to Yosemite National Park in California
with Ansel Adams, David McAlpin, and Godfrey and
Helen Rockefeller.

1939

February: The Dole Pineapple Company commissions
O'Keeffe to travel to Hawaii and produce pictures of
pineapples. She later travels on her own to Maui to
paint landscapes.

April: O'Keeffe is honored as one of the twelve most accomplished women of the last fifty years at the New York World's Fair.

1940

October: O'Keeffe purchases her first property, Rancho de los Burros, at Ghost Ranch.

1943

The first retrospective of O'Keeffe's art, *Georgia O'Keeffe's Paintings: 1915-1941*, is held at the Art Institute of Chicago.

1945

After many years of negotiating, O'Keeffe purchases an abandoned hacienda on three acres of land in Abiquiú, New Mexico, from the Archdiocese of Santa Fe.

1946

May 14: The Museum of Modern Art holds a retrospective

of O'Keeffe's paintings, the first solo show to honor
a woman.

July 13: Alfred Stieglitz dies. O'Keeffe spends the major-
ity of the next two years in New York settling his
estate.

1947

O'Keeffe helps organize a special exhibition of Stieglitz's
collection at the Museum of Modern Art that travels
to the Art Institute of Chicago.

O'Keeffe visits Taliesin West, Frank Lloyd Wright's winter
home and school in Scottsdale, Arizona.

1948

From the patio of her Abiquiú home, O'Keeffe paints the
first abstractions centered on the *salita* (little room)
door.

1949

After leaving New York, O'Keeffe makes New Mexico her
permanent home, dividing her time between Abiquiú

in winter and spring and Ghost Ranch in summer
and fall.

O'Keeffe is elected to the National Institute of Arts and
Letters.

1951

O'Keeffe begins to travel internationally, first to Mexico
with writer Spud Johnson. In Mexico City, she
meets famed muralist Diego Rivera and his wife and
painter, Frida Kahlo, later traveling to the Yucatán
with Rosa and Miguel Covarrubias.

1952

Edith Halpert's Downtown Gallery hosts O'Keeffe's first
solo exhibition in the space.

1953

O'Keeffe visits Europe for the first time, traveling to
France, Germany, and Spain.

February: The retrospective exhibition *Georgia O'Keeffe:
Paintings* opens at the Dallas Museum of Fine Arts.

1954

O'Keeffe travels to Spain for three months.

1956

O'Keeffe travels to Peru for three months, where she
is inspired to paint landscapes and closely cropped
paintings of the wall of Sacsayhuamán in the city of
Cusco.

1959

O'Keeffe makes the first of several trips around the
world, visiting Japan, Hong Kong, India, Singapore,
Southeast Asia, Egypt, Iran, Syria, Israel, and Rome.
She begins a series of paintings of the earth and sky
based on her view from airplanes.

1960

O'Keeffe travels for six weeks to Japan, Taiwan, Hong
Kong, and other destinations in Asia and the Pacific
Islands.

1961

At age seventy-three, O'Keeffe rafts the Colorado River on a ten-day trip through Glen Canyon with Todd Webb, Eliot Porter, and other friends.

1962

The American Academy of Arts and Letters elects O'Keeffe as a member.

1963

O'Keeffe travels to Greece, Egypt, and the Near East.

1965

O'Keeffe creates the largest painting of her career, *Sky Above the Clouds IV* (1965, 96 × 288 in.), in her garage at Ghost Ranch.

1966

The Art Museum at the University of New Mexico in Albuquerque presents the first solo exhibition of O'Keeffe's work in her adopted state.

March: The Amon Carter Museum of Western Art in Fort Worth, Texas, presents *Georgia O'Keeffe: An Exhibition of the Work of the Artist from 1915 to 1966.*

1967

Vogue magazine publishes an article about O'Keeffe describing her work as an antecedent to color field abstraction. Cecil Beaton provides photographs for the spread, featuring O'Keeffe in a black kimono.

The School of the Art Institute of Chicago awards O'Keeffe an honorary doctorate.

1968

Life magazine features O'Keeffe on the cover, "Georgia O'Keeffe in New Mexico: Stark Visions of a Pioneer Painter."

1969

O'Keeffe is named a Benjamin Franklin Fellow by the Royal Society for the Encouragement of Arts, Manufactures, and Commerce, London.

O'Keeffe travels to Austria.

1970

The National Institute of Arts and Letters awards
    O'Keeffe the gold medal in painting.

October: O'Keeffe installs her retrospective *Georgia
    O'Keeffe* at the Whitney Museum of American Art.

1971

Macular degeneration begins to affect O'Keeffe's central
    vision. She can only see peripherally.

1972

O'Keeffe completes her last unassisted oil painting,
    The Beyond, and stops painting for four years.

1973

O'Keeffe meets the sculptor Juan Hamilton, who later
    becomes her friend, assistant, and representative.

1974

The Governor's Gallery at the New Mexico State Capitol
    exhibits O'Keeffe's paintings of New Mexico in her
    second solo exhibition in the state.

O'Keeffe's agent Doris Bry edits *Some Memories of Drawings*, a book on her drawings from 1915–63, published with O'Keeffe's words by the University of New Mexico Press.

O'Keeffe travels to Morocco.

1976

O'Keeffe begins painting again.

Viking Press publishes a monograph titled *Georgia O'Keeffe*, featuring 108 reproductions and an autobiographical text.

O'Keeffe travels to Antigua.

1977

President Gerald R. Ford presents O'Keeffe with the Medal of Freedom.

Perry Miller Adato's film, *Georgia O'Keeffe*, is shown on National Public Television.

1978

Georgia O'Keeffe: A Portrait by Alfred Stieglitz opens at the
  Metropolitan Museum of Art. O'Keeffe writes the
  catalog, including many previously unpublished
  images.

1979

O'Keeffe travels to Costa Rica and Guatemala.

1980

With encouragement from Hamilton, O'Keeffe begins to
  create clay pots.

Laurie Lisle publishes *Portrait of an Artist: A Biography of
  Georgia O'Keeffe.*

1982

May: O'Keeffe Returns to Hawaii.

O'Keeffe creates her final abstract sculpture, *Abstraction,*
  measuring eleven feet high, which is included in
  a show of American sculptors at the San Francisco
  Museum of Modern Art.

1983

O'Keeffe makes her last international trip, to Costa Rica.

1984

O'Keeffe moves from Abiquiú to Santa Fe.

1985

President Ronald Reagan presents O'Keeffe with the
National Medal of Arts.

1986

March 6: Georgia O'Keefe dies at St. Vincent's Hospital in
Santa Fe. Her ashes are scattered at the peak of Cerro
Pedernal, a mesa near her home.

ACKNOWLEDGMENTS

First and foremost, my sincere gratitude to Georgia O'Keeffe, whose indomitable spirit and inspiring words create the foundation of this publication. It is a true privilege to play a part in honoring her legacy.

I extend my deepest thanks as well to the outstanding team at the Georgia O'Keeffe Museum, with special thanks to Cody Hartley, Liz O'Brien, and Bonnie Steward. Your dedication and expert archival management made this book possible.

As always, I am eternally grateful to the entire team at Princeton University Press for their unwavering support and commitment to excellence. My very special thanks to Michelle Komie, Christie Henry, Terri O'Prey, Cathy Slovensky, Jacqueline Poirier, Colleen Suljic, Laurie Schlesinger, Cathy Felgar, Jodi Price, Alexandria Leonard, Karen Corvello, Tony Lutkus, Annie Miller, and Bob Bettendorf. Your continued professionalism, passion, and collaboration have been instrumental in realizing this and many other projects over the years.

I am deeply grateful as well to Lisa Volpe, Malcolm Daniel, and Howard and Pat Farber for their support.

A special thank you to editorial director Fiona Graham for her leadership in guiding this project and the entire ISMs series. My thanks also goes to Susan Delson for her thoughtful and discerning editorial guidance.

Warm thanks as well to Taliesin Thomas and Steven Rodríguez for their ongoing support.

Above all, I give all my bottomless gratitude to my amazing wife, Abbey, and to my wonderful children, Justin, Ethan, Ellie, and Jonah, for their love and encouragement.

As always, I give endless love and thanks to my mother, Judith.

LARRY WARSH

JUNE 2025

ILLUSTRATIONS

Frontispiece: Alfred Stieglitz. *Georgia O'Keeffe*, 1928.
Gelatin silver print, $4^{5}/_{8} \times 3^{9}/_{16}$ inches. Georgia O'Keeffe
Museum. Gift of The Georgia O'Keeffe Foundation.
[2003.1.13]

Page 118: Georgia O'Keeffe. *Horse's Skull with White
Rose*, 1931. Oil on canvas, $30^{1}/_{16} \times 16^{1}/_{8}$ inches. Georgia
O'Keeffe Museum. Gift of Anne Windfohr Grimes, Anne
Windfohr Marion, and Anne Burnett Tandy. © Georgia
O'Keeffe Museum. [2021.8.1]

Georgia O'Keeffe is one of the most significant artists of the twentieth century, renowned for her contribution to modern art. Born on November 15, 1887, the second of seven children, Georgia Totto O'Keeffe grew up on a farm near Sun Prairie, Wisconsin. By the time she graduated from high school in 1905, O'Keeffe had determined to make her way as an artist.

By the mid-1920s, O'Keeffe was recognized as one of America's most important and successful artists, known for her paintings of New York skyscrapers—an essentially American symbol of modernity—as well as her equally radical depictions of flowers and the desert of New Mexico.

The Georgia O'Keeffe Museum's collections include nearly 150 paintings and hundreds of works on paper (pencil and charcoal drawings, as well as pastels and watercolors). Her work is also in the permanent collections of many major institutions, including the Metropolitan Museum of Art, the Museum of Modern Art, New York, the Art Institute of Chicago, Amon Carter Museum of American Art, the Brooklyn Museum, and the Milwaukee Art Museum, among many others.

Larry Warsh has been active in the art world for over thirty years as a publisher and artist-collaborator. An early collector of Keith Haring and Jean-Michel Basquiat, Warsh was a lead organizer for the exhibition *Basquiat: The Unknown Notebooks*, which debuted at the Brooklyn Museum, New York, in 2015 and continues to travel to international museums. He has loaned artworks by Haring and Basquiat from his collection to numerous exhibitions worldwide and he served as a curatorial consultant on *Keith Haring | Jean-Michel Basquiat: Crossing Lines* for the National Gallery of Victoria, Melbourne. The founder of *Museums Magazine*, Warsh has been involved in numerous publishing projects and is the editor of several titles published by Princeton University Press, including the -isms series, *Jean-Michel Basquiat: The Notebooks* (2017), *Keith Haring: 31 Subway Drawings* (2021), *James Rosenquist: Collages, Drawings, and Paintings in Process* (2024), *Wassily Kandinsky: The Sketchbooks* (2025), and two books by Ai Weiwei, *Humanity* (2018) and *Weiwei-isms* (2012). Warsh has served on the board of the Getty Museum Photographs Council and was a founding member of the Basquiat Authentication Committee from 1993 until its dissolution in 2012.

ISMs

Larry Warsh, Series Editor

The ISMs series distills the voices of an exciting range of visual artists and designers into captivating, beautifully made books of quotations for a new generation of readers. In turn passionate, inspiring, humorous, witty, and challenging, these collections offer powerful statements on topics ranging from contemporary culture, politics, and race, to creativity, humanity, and the role of art in the world. Books in this series are edited by Larry Warsh and published by Princeton University Press in association with No More Rulers.

O'Keeffe-isms, Georgia O'Keeffe

Duchamp-isms, Marcel Duchamp

Obrist-isms, Hans Ulrich Obrist

Calder-isms, Alexander Calder

Ono-isms, Yoko Ono

Minter-isms, Marilyn Minter

Fairey-isms, Shepard Fairey